To Jim & Fiona & family
Best wishes
Juan & family

El Campo

El Campo

Poems by
Juan Delgado

Paintings by
Simón Silva

CAPRA PRESS
SANTA BARBARA

DEDICATION

Para mi amigo Juan Delgado y a todos las personas que me han brindado su apoyo.
– SIMÓN SILVA

To my friends, my other family.
– JUAN DELGADO

Grateful acknowledgment is made to the following periodicals in which
early versions of poems originally appeared:

"Campesinos" in *Borderlands: Texas Poetry Review,* No. 8 1996
"I-5 Incident" and "Gastado" in *Borderlands: Texas Poetry Review,* No. 9 1997

A version of "Mercado del Aire" first appeared in Juan Delgado's *Green Web,*
published by The University of Georgia Press, 1994.

Cover design and book design by Frank Goad, Santa Barbara
Cover painting by Simón Silva

LIBRARY OF CONGRESS CATALOGING-IN-PUBLICATION DATA

Delgado, Juan. 1960-
El campo : poems & paintings / Juan Delgado & Simón Silva.
p. cm.
ISBN 0-88496-428-0 (paper : alk. paper)
I. Silva, Simón. II. Title.
PS3554.E442465E4 1998
811' .54—dc21
97-46495
CIP

Capra Press
Post Office Box 2068
Santa Barbara, CA 93120

CONTENTS

CHUPAROSA

The feeder is red with sugared water.
A hummingbird's wings burn.

Behind a window with bars
a man lies face down on a cot;
his chest beats out a dream
while the hummingbird hovers.

The dreamer sips at what
his eyes offer him: the U.S. border.
Poking his face through
an opening in the chain-link fence,
he checks if it's safe to cross.

The possibility of work is his nectar.
He dashes into a ravine
and lies flat on the ground;
he has made it past the patrols.

His dream is the hummingbird's flight.
His eyes scan the night.
If he is not spotted, he will join the rest,
but the desert is a sweeping net.

CLASS WORK

They return in their flour-sack dresses
and oversized hand-me-downs in mid year,
dusting off the fields in the hallway
before knocking at their classroom door.

While the teacher sits them at a table
and hands them paper, crayons, and books,
the rest chatter and fidget in their rows
until told to stop and get to their work.

He presses a page flat and reads to them,
underlining each word with his index finger,
tracing a line the children's eyes follow
while they repeat: "Jane runs after a ball."

In his broken Spanish he tells the children
around the table that he wants them to draw
a picture of Jane running in her yard.
He returns to the front of the class.

One boy draws a girl striding over a cloud
after an apple suspended in front of her.
The apple is red as sin, and the girl is Eve.
The green cloud is heaven he tells another.

"No! Estúpido," says a girl who returns
to drawing her figures by placing her paper
over the page and tracing out the figures,
then coloring Jane's long hair yellow.

At lunch, among the stacked food trays,
they fold their brown bags into their pockets
and run on the blacktop until they hear
the bells calling them into their lines.

A few take deep breaths, tired from swinging
on bars, and others stomp their boots clean
while the teacher ushers them into the room,
pointing to their unfinished work on the table,
their versions of a girl in a green paradise.

INSIDE A TRUCK SHELL

Ahora, Juan, this road your boss has you on leads
to your wife, Anna, and to Alfonso, your boy,
this road that also means money. Juan, what will you
do when your boss stops his truck and opens the door?
Will you jump out, glad to work for another day,
glad to work hard so you can forget those you have
left behind, ready with your lunch in your hand, so
he can point you in the direction of your work?
Juan Camacho, you shit—go home, surprise Anna.
Right now, Chata, your crazy neighbor, is asking
your wife for salt, and Pepe, the baker, is drunk.
The girls next door are combing their hair, and your son,
Juan, where is your son? What is he doing? Think, Juan.
Ask your boss to stop his truck. You have your lunch,
just walk on the freeway in any direction,
it does not matter—the border patrol will spot
you, take you back to Tijuana for free, from there
you will get a train—think. He is parking his truck.
He always drags his boots; no doubt he is also
loosening the belt around his gut and lifting
his pants up, spitting his last sip of cold coffee.
He always fumbles putting the key in the lock.
The door is open—what will you do, *ahora*?

GASTADO

The rows he irrigates
appear in his ceiling,
the cracks in the stucco.
He lies on his bed,
a lump of earth that rises,
shaped by the spinning
of another working day
in El Norte.

In the fields his hand
is a shovel that flows
with the water soaking
into the rows he mans.
The sun bakes him
the brown of his pueblo,
the pottery shaped by
his ancestors' hands.

He traces his palm,
looking for a route
past the field and work
he's learned to do so well,
but by the day's end
he's a broken pot
with half of its pieces
pointing the way home.

UNA FLOR

Rosario works by the freeway.
The stems in her bucket stir
the water muddy, calling up
the father she ran away from.
A cluster of car lights brake,
the engines idling at the light.
The road narrows to a blacktop
that slithers through the city.

She holds a sunflower to a car
and asks: "Flores, Señor?"
A man glances at her the way
he did at a dog crossing his path.
He taps his steering wheel,
eyes fixed on the road, a trail
of oily spots he'll park over
before he closes his garage.

A horn begins yelling: "Green!"
The billboard model stretches into
a mountain range of skin,
smoothed into a luster.
Back home in Guatemala,
Rosario is the family's spinster,
left on a kitchen shelf, a dish
her father tried to polish.

She is the troubled daughter
he waits for; once as a girl
she peered over his shoulder
while he played a game of poker.

Only the rich could sit
around his table and play.
They noticed a drunk Indio
staggering up the church steps.

Her father bet the drunk would fall
before reaching the statue
of Bartolomé de las Casas.
He did collapse, reciting his prayers.
She saw a stream of blood,
a prayer running down his chin,
his swollen lips carnation red.
His eyelids were half closed.

He lifted his head and propped
himself up with a hand, then another.
He sat, his head swaying back.
The men around the table laughed.
With her father fixed on the kitty
she toppled his table and ran,
weaving through the market,
pushing the tables in her way.

Her father's flicking wrist,
the way he tossed his cards,
is another rush of cars,
their hubcaps, rattling coins.
She sees his poker face
behind a shaded glass.
His hubcaps whirl backward,
speeding toward the next light.

VELORIO

Sal digs a hole deep as a man.
He stops shoveling, grabs a pickax
so he can claw through the clay
and find the bloated sewage pipe.
Raising the pickax, he swings
like a man planning an escape.

His pickax pierces through metal,
a gas line, the stench of a pig's pen.
Light-headed now, drunk with fatigue,
deep in his day's work, he thinks
he's found his plugged-up pipe
and whirls back for a final strike.

A spark from his blow wakes the street,
and it makes dogs cower away.
It rattles the glass of window frames.
It spills coffee and burns, then a voice
turns to a door and says, "What the hell?"

Above him his guardian angels gather;
one throws his head back and sings.
Another strums his guitar and joins in.
The accordion fills its belly with air
and squeezes out the tune of Sal's death.
The dogs of the street begin to bark,
sniffing at the air for his scent.

AWAKENED IN A FIELD

I made car batteries new,
replacing their dead cells.
And once one exploded
on our work bench;
its acid ran down the wall,
a fire that peeled the paint,
a name with a heart beside it,
and a few phone numbers.
I carried your photo
inside my coat pocket
when I left for Stockton.
Now from a bed of corn husks,
I rise and brush the silk
away from my face and work.
My hands are heavy as clay.
My fellow workers are gone,
some to other fields and work;
a few returned to Mexico,
to their wives and children.
Did your father make it
through another dry season?
Is your brother leaving
the farm and coming up north?
I have work until summer,
so write when you receive this.
I loaded the corn in boxes
all day yesterday and today,
but between the company store
and the bar in town I can't
seem to save any money,
so I can't mail you anything.
Forgive me for leaving you,
for thinking I had to go.

15

CAMPESINOS

A foreman drives by the fields counting his pickers,
their spines bent like the necks of clothes hangers.
What hangs on them is the harvest, the fields
and roads from crop to crop merging into
a circuit of hands working close to the ground.
Others are packing the cabbages into a truck,
cramping the boxes the way their coyote had them
hidden in his camper shell crossing the border;
he smuggled ten of them, his crop of wetbacks.
They sat, their heads rocking into a half-sleep
until a voice woke them, their new foreman,
calling and directing them to a line of tents.
Some tents had cots, old army surplus,
and others, the trash of the last field hands.

A driver starts his route with the packed cabbages,
coming upon tire tracks that went off the road.
The wreckage of a van is fenced off
with yellow tape, and the bodies on the ground
are covered with yellow sheets, a yellow unlike
any bush or stone viewed through a windshield.
The police direct traffic, waving the truck on,
and at a pothole a few cabbages fall,
a faceless green pushed aside.
The driver sees in his rearview mirror
the scattered bodies again, a receding yellow.
Their journey was a wrinkled map unfolding
a country shaded by the promise of work,
inviting as hands on a wheel, an open road.

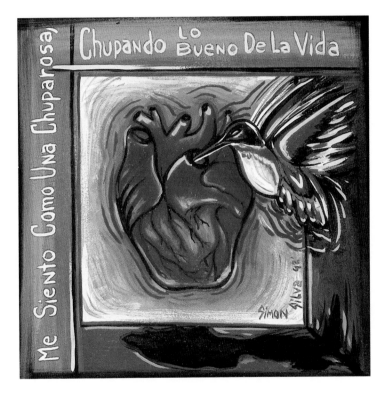

"Chuparosa"
Gouache, 6"x 6"

"Amor Eterno"
Gouache, 28"x 30"

"De Sol a Sol"
Oil, 24"x 36"

"Los Compadres"
Oil, 24"x 36"

"Una Flor"
Gouache, 12"x 12"

"Familia"
Oil, 17"x 20"

"Campesino # 1"
Oil, 30"x 40"

"Amor de Padre"
Oil, 24"x 36"

CON LOS PÁJAROS

I sat under my father's clothesline,
a web of ropes tied to four-by-fours
jutting unevenly out of the ground.
I saw the sky in muddy puddles,
the dripping of sleeves and skirts.

Like a pot, our street simmered.
Our neighbor's face in the kitchen window
disappeared behind a raised pot lid.
Her girl peered, then moved to the table
once she saw her mother cool down
the spoon, the first taste of supper.
When father arrived, he untied the bandana
around his neck, the day's sweat.
He leaned on his truck, and I noticed
the line of clothes sagging, tired as limbs.

On Saturday we finished our house.
I mixed the stucco, shoveled it into a bucket,
carried it on my shoulder up a ladder
to where he dug in with his trowel and worked.
Pressing the stucco into the chicken wire
and smoothing it out, he stopped to recite:
"We're just a coat of stucco away."
I mixed until a coat finished the wall,
drying with the odor of moist soil.

Once his hands returned with the birds.
His song was a bundle of carrots caked
by dirt, dark as his palms at dusk.

BREAKING AWAY

One field's strawberries are unfit,
undersized for the stores' display counters.
A loss for the grower, but for the family
of pickers, they are sweet, extra money.

They will try to sell them by the roadside.
The back of their van will turn into a stall.
They pack the fruit, sliding the boxes past
the rolled-out mattress, the boy's bed.

On the ride home the fruit's odor weaves
around the boy, flutters in the van's curtains,
returns to him, and enters his dream: He picks,
his hand pinching off a strawberry's stem.

The shadows of his hands darken and flap,
turning into a pair of wings, the crow's.
They glide beyond the rows and workers
who must keep pace for the rows ahead.

Their hands are chapped, the over-tilled soil.
The crow peers under his wing at the field
dwindling to a green square and squawks.
He is not bound to the road or the seasons.

DANDELION

He is going to stop thinking
about his crooked teeth,
about all the rattling his truck
makes circling the golf course
while passing her country club home.
So, she is rich, so he
is her gardener, so he is
the Mexican, so what
he says to himself—he will go
to her pool, get courage
from its mouth of light and wait for
her sign, the way crabgrass
hides its roots when it is weeded,
and he assures himself
endurance will be his beauty.
When the pool is shadows,
she waves him on from her window.
He rubs and cleans his teeth
with a dirty finger, then spits,
walking to her front door.
Only self-doubt can kill a weed.

I-5 INCIDENT
"Hit-run victim survives four days alone."

On the fourth day the phone wires talked,
replied like voices pressed to pillows,
trapped behind walls or dying in the wind,
then quiet as a priest who listens to sins.
All sorts of things I imagined; they kept me going.
No. I didn't see the car; I had my back to it.
I only heard its radio, you know,
American rock and roll. No.
I wasn't crossing; I stayed to the side.
When struck, I hit the rushing ground
and dragged myself toward the bushes
of an embankment, afraid they'd return.
In La Sagrada Familia, my neighborhood,
a man delivering Coke on his bike
fell at a corner and lifted his head
only to vanish under a city bus,
so I wasn't going near the road again.
Plus, I couldn't. Look at my legs.
My jeans were soaked in blood.
Dirt stuck to them. I patted my legs,
thinking they were part of the ground.
I was half dead, a lizard without a tail.
Luckily, I had the sprinkler's water;
its head was broken. I held its cool neck,
but my stomach groaned, all knotted up.
I shouted when I heard a car coming
and shook the bushes at the headlights.
Through the night I held on to a branch
and had a dream about a market place
where people drifted among the stalls.

Some glanced, keeping up with the crowd;
others haggled, then turned from the vendors,
walking away, seemingly losing interest.
I came upon a stall of toys: race cars,
dolls with eyes bright as hubcaps,
and puppets hooked, their limbs still
as if they had fallen through the sky.
A child stopped to tug the string of one
and tried to get his mother's attention
by having it dance and wave its arm,
but she was already several stalls ahead,
looking in front for him, shouting his name.
He ran, dodging strangers and yelling, "Wait!"
I heard his voice over the crowd's
and woke to a semi and the rush of wind
that made the oleander's leaves tremble.

RAUL

Poor Raul, why did you tell
our boss after cashing your check
you were going to Joel's Studio in town
to get a portrait of yourself?
He only laughed at you, then at me
for agreeing to take you there.
"That's a good one. Crazy wetbacks,"
he murmured, handing us our checks.
He doesn't care if I'm fifty
and that you're only a kid
as long as we work hard.

He doesn't care about your sick mother
in Mexico, who longs for a photo
of you to hang in her bedroom,
but I do. Trust me, Raul.
While we tried to keep warm
on our mattress with one blanket,
you told me you were a man
and not to try any funny business,
but you should've acted like one
and kept to yourself and never hid
your money in this shack we sleep in
that smells like a chicken coop.

Our camp is full of thieves.
You can start with our boss.
Your own kind can be the worst,
full of poison like those tanks
outside by the grapefruit trees.
I knew a foreman in Yuba who had
his way with boys like you,

then he cut them up
and fed them back to the soil.
Raul, beware of a smiling face
and what's hiding behind it.

On Saturday, you greased your hair
and left behind your baseball cap,
its brim soiled, a circuit
of crops we picked together.
Remember our first time?
Your bare knees were so dirty.
Your hands reached for the artichokes
and cut their heads off the stems.
You couldn't imagine people eating them.
I said they were white people's nopales.
I could've taught you how to eat them.
You needed me back then.
You couldn't even handle a knife.
I taught you how to hold it,
so you wouldn't tire your wrist.

Your bones are so delicate;
I recall you once found a harmless snake
that wrapped itself around your wrist.
Its eye was a mirror, a glare.
It reminded me of a black sun,
black as our boss' stare.
I've seen how he looks at you.

Yesterday you checked your hair
at every store window and mirror
we passed on our way.
At the studio you took a number.
I stared at the portraits on the walls

and recalled the photos of the dead
I saw pinned at the entrance
of a village church I once visited.
The photos' corners had curled.
The faces in them had yellowed
to the wax of the altar's candles.
I joked that taking your photo
would bring you bad luck
and laughed at the worry in your face.
But you smiled at the calling of your number.
You stood by a cake of plaster,
rigid as its electric candle.

Why didn't you tell me it was
your birthday? Imagine my surprise.
Did you think I would've laughed
like our boss? Trust me, I wouldn't have.
You should've told me—now look:
your special day has flashed by,
a snuffed out candle, over like that.
After you posed,
I saw you tug at your sweater,
having almost outgrown it.
When your mother gets her photos,
she'll see your budding manhood.
You moved for the girl next in line.
Her dress was rich as ice cream.
Your lips were dry from smiling.
We left, walking in the noon sun.
You were thirsty, a half-exposed root,
trying to guess what was ahead.
Raul, you can't go on like this,
living on the surface of your days.

ASH WEDNESDAY

A girl slides her hand into her mother's
and turns from the evening sun, seeing their shadows
lean away from their feet, cross the sidewalk,
and rise on a wall.

Half of them floats behind like ghosts
following them to church.
At the entrance a cross stretches into a tree,
its branches bare.

Her mother will pray for a good season of crops.
By the door a saint is embedded into the wall,
his upright casket, where he listens for footsteps
with closed eyes.

The girl leans into her mother's hip,
afraid he might peel his stone eyelids open.

WINGS

I. Putting in the Hours

Sylvia spots in the grapevines a nest,
empty, unraveling, half-detached,
and imagines a set of eggs balanced
in the nest's palm.

After the plane finishes its runs,
her throat is cotton ball dry.
The spray absorbed in the leaves
is sticky to the touch.

She reties her bandana over her mouth,
feeling her stomach, the kick of her child.

2. Grapes

The working ant was sprayed and wore it,
a coating thick as honey, and he zigzagged
on a scent trail with a crumb on his head.
The bird pecking the grapes flew it
back to the nest, lodged in her throat.

The woman at the store who bought them
didn't know they held it in their peel.
She polished one, thrilling her,
the taste of its sugar.

3. His Limbs Are Springs

Carlos is placed on his rocking horse,
facing the grapevines his family works.
He balances himself with only his head,
the reins resting on his horse's neck.

His horse flies above a row of trees,
a sharecropper making a run over the fields.
The children picking alongside their parents
hear his laughter, his horse's springs.

4. Sylvia's Garden

With knees of ash she works her plot,
weeding a patch of stubborn crabgrass.
She pulls out clumps, then digs up roots,
white as ivory.

Head down, a leaf in the midday sun,
she shapes the soil into rims for watering
and leaves behind a line of seeds,
vivid, a nest of opening mouths.

MERCADO DEL AIRE

I lower the burner, noticing a cut on my hand;
how quickly I withdrew my hand yesterday
after noticing it beneath the cashier's light.
On my radio a man announces a miracle cream
that vanishes warts and for no extra money
he'll throw in a tea that helps you lose weight.
Then a woman gets on begging to know
if her deported boyfriend has returned to the States
and repeats a number in case he hears her plea.
I look at the lunch bags I've packed so far.
Another woman trades her sewing machine
for a ticket to Tijuana, saying she's had enough.
Someone jumps out of bed, dashes to the bathroom
while the others drift into my kitchen, hungry.

Once the bartering is over, and they're gone,
I sing along with my radio; a lover throws pebbles
at a window, striking a chord that announces love.
With another song I recall my sister dancing
around a rooster that pecked at her heels
as she pinned the wash to our clothesline.
As I stir, I imagine in my pot's mouth the plaza
where my sister and I walked by the admiring boys,
the ones who hid in a field of sunflowers
and watched us rinsing our hair, heavy with water.
Their eyes were the eyes of the bougainvillea.
I get some flour and sprinkle it with water,
rolling the sticky dough into a village I long for
before the pot lid starts to steam and dance.

WHISPERING A NIGHTMARE OVER A WALL

I washed my children's hands;
the river swirled around my knees.
Cleaning the face of Luz, my girl,
I turned my back on my son
who spotted a floating pine cone
then took a step, then another.

I could see only the cone
drifting among the rocks.
I plunged my hand, finding
a root yanked by the current.
I decided to swim downriver
and yelled for Luz to stay put.

The river carried me away
for what seemed a lifetime,
the trees blurring into shade.
It took me toward the sea
where I kept on searching,
trying to find where he hid.

I found myself on a white shore.
The waves approached like voices.
Looking behind a beached log
I spotted footprints in the sand
and noticed Luz was also playing
an endless game of hide-and-seek.

LA LLORONA

1. Moon

Two girls walk to the river bank,
the yucca plants pointing the way.
Wiggling their toes in the sand,
they decide to swim toward the moon.
Their hands flutter above their heads;
the moon turns them into butterflies
gliding over the surface and reeds.
In the morning their bodies appear
where the laundry dries on the rocks.
The people have no one to blame
but the woman who walks the river.
They say she drowned her own son.
She sang him lullabies; he floated
like a lily until he could not hear
her song and feel his hand in hers.

2. Water

The clarity of the moon
begins to sway the reeds,
her children's hair.
She sees her children drift
into an eddy, swirl in moss,
the water's flesh.
She retraces her path, the steps
that led her children to the lake.
Her story is like water:
it takes the shape of the holder,
a storyteller's mouth.
She dips her hands and drinks.
Their voices fill her throat.

3. The Widening Sea

The pier she is on goes beyond
the waves to the rising swells.
Her clenched hands no longer feel
the strain of pushing the stroller.
She tucks in her baby's blanket,
then walks to the sounds of wheels
against the planks and the calls
of seagulls that whirl and scream.
A nylon line is tied to the rail
and dangles over the edge.
It vanishes, pointing to the sea.
She lifts her baby over the rail
and lets the bundle drop, undraping.
A gull gives chase to the wing,
the blanket's flapping corner.
She looks at the ripples, the ocean's
widening mouth, then she leaps,
her legs as stiff as a baby doll's.
With little light reaching the bottom,
her body darkens, half of her
a reported story, the rest a myth,
retold, shifting with the tide.

SUNBURNT

Bloated from over drinking water,
I stop to notice my mother drag
her bucket of apricots past my ladder.
We are late in picking the fruit;
some apricots are sunburnt,
their skin hardened to a brown,
reminding me of my birth mark.
Many have dropped, picked by birds,
and lay bruised on the ground
where flies hover over them.
Licking a finger wet, I clean
my cheek, dirty as a fallen apricot,
and climb, thinking I can't see
the ripest from inside the tree.
I duck my head, weave my hand
among branches, reaching for apricots,
snatching them, careful not to squeeze.
Branches prick and snare my shirt
when I steady myself against them.
I imagine being caught in a web,
trying to avoid the sun's glare,
then I go on, reaching for more.

"Un Día de Campo"
Gouache, 17"x 29"

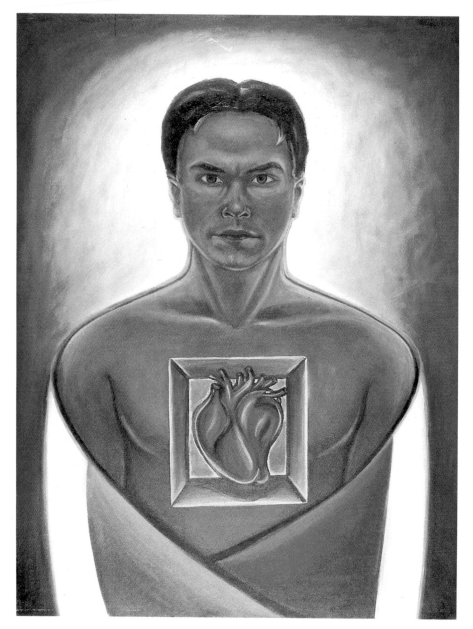

"Hecho en México" (Self-portrait)
Oil, 22"x 28"

"El Cumpleaños"
Oil, 24"x 36"

43

"Amor a Todas Horas"
Gouache, 20"x 25"

"El Lonche"
Oil, 24"x 36"

"Dos Mujeres"
Gouache, 21"x 27"

"La Llorona"
Oil, 24"x 36"

"Las Comadres"
Gouache, 24"x 24"

HER FLOWERS

1.
Indifferent to her and her sunflower,
Mr. Russell, her teacher, paces and states
the date the Civil War was over.
He stands, rereading the history book,
distrusting the words he reads out loud.
She draws, then shades and darkens
a face, as wide as a cut-out heart,
with jagged petals, large as ears.
The petals flame around the face.
Again, Mr. Russell paces the aisles,
holding the heavy text in his good hand,
the other wilted since childhood.
She fingers her drawing and smudges
the slender stem of her flower gray.

2.
She traces her hand, another flower
that thrives beneath an arc of lead,
crowned with rays that fly off the page.
A snaking hose appears and soaks
the shadow leaning from her flower;
its petals begin to open, counting down.
She waits for the hallways to fill,
for kids to spill out of the gates
into the parking lot, into the streets,
swinging their books by their sides.
She leaves the sky a paper white,
and draws herself among more faces.
She stands in a field of sunflowers,
their tongues ripening in their shells.

SCARECROW

Among the rows the birds hop and peck,
hungry for the strawberries' seeds.
I gather a PVC pipe from a ditch,
a large branch shaped like a wishbone,
and other scraps swept onto the field.

I fasten rags onto a wire chest held up
by the branch I planted and secured with stones.
I poke the pipe through for the arms
and place a glove at one end,
watching it catch the wind.
A rolled up shirt I pat into a head,
tying its sleeves back, a blindfold.

I walk to the field's edge, by the highway,
watching my scarecrow lean in the wind.
The birds circle in with their eyes of tar.
A motorist honks at me, at my scarecrow's
flapping clothing and his waving hand.

I stand, half admiring his effort, but prepared
for it to fall, a bundle inviting the birds
like the Santa Ana winds that rip and carry
away the plastic sheets from over the seedlings.
Drivers keep turning their faces toward us.

Yesterday, in the freeway's middle divider
I spotted a man with a bag over his shoulder.
His hand pressed down on his cowboy hat.
His eyes a brim of shade, his jaw clenched.

His unkempt beard turned away, and he was
eyeing the distance he had to cross.
The highway's guardrail raced beside me
and surged ahead to the man and beyond.

The rush of black, a ripped tire tread.
He took a step, not glancing at me, or the rest
of the fast approaching cars before he ran
across four lanes and into the oleanders.

He had kicked up his knees to get speed,
the canvas bag bouncing off his back.
I had clenched the wheel, glanced in my mirror,
and tried not to overreact, my foot over the pedal.

Afraid to change lanes, I stared ahead,
cornered by my speed and the rush-hour traffic.
Above me an interchange sprawled out its limbs,
its off-ramps and on-ramps rising and falling.

I don't know why I honked after his dash,
turning back to see only the bush stir.
The steady sound of wheels on gravel
was like a river after a downpour
that overflows and surrounds me.

THE OPOSSUM

All morning my crew of chainsaws hacked
at the grove of unwanted grapefruit trees
then at the surrounding eucalyptus trees, once a wall,
a windbreaker for the Santa Ana winds
that could clean the fruit right off a branch.

By noon the citrus trees were piles
of tangled branches and trunks left sliced
small enough to toss into my truck bed.
I had my crew thin out the fallen brush.

Luis, the foreman of my crew, exaggerated
his steps as he walked over the branches,
his blade cutting a path, but he stopped
by the side of a tree, facing an opossum.

He kept his chainsaw at her face,
the chain screaming around its bar.
Eyes tiny and black as tacks stared at him.
With her ears pricked to the whirling blade,
she growled back, showing her teeth.

The roar of his chainsaw did his talking,
then he stepped aside, letting her through,
and behind her stepped three more, her litter,
in single file, their fur white as hers.
Leisurely they walked off, sun-blinded.

We watched the last tail slither into the brush.
I said I wasn't paying him to stand around.
We walked to the last standing eucalyptus tree.
Their oily leaves and bark had scented our clothing.
Luis said they made medicine from the leaves.

I had Luis climb the eucalyptus and cut.
With a wide belt wrapped around the trunk and him,
he dug his spiked heels deeper into the wood.
The upper branches fell in thumps, shaking the ground.

Then with a bulldozer I toppled the trunk,
its stump clenching the roots like a dirty fist.
Its heaved-up system of roots seemed not dense
enough to have ever kept such a tree upright.

I ordered Luis to begin cutting through its trunk,
twisted, resting on a large branch and when
his blade went through, the trunk snapped back,
jerking the blade into Luis' face, into an eye.
We put him in my truck bed and drove for help.

I held him down, covered his eye, a rag of blood.
Behind the blind one he kept saying he saw
her growl, her teeth jagged as his blade.
I kept him calm, repeating we're almost there,
feeling the heavy rag drip when I pressed
with the scent of eucalyptus on my hands.

CHRISTINE

Dad's in our truck,
sleeping off last night's beer;
he left me working. I hate onions.
I'll never get the smell out of my hands,
even if I rinse with lemon juice.
Dad can't even begin to understand
that the ends of my hair are all frayed
like the shoe laces on my old boots.
And what about my school clothes?
I bet the day before school begins,
he'll take me to Sears and walk right up
to a rack, the one with all the red tags.
He'll pull the first thing he sees,
put this gross dress next to me
and say: "Hey, that looks good."
Then he'll go look at the tools,
saying: "Here, thirty dollars. Don't forget
to get yourself some socks and underwear."
He'll do it to me again—drop me off
at the office, tell the lady behind the counter
he thinks I should be in the fifth grade.
He'll leave me filling out the forms
next to some kid who wipes his nose
on his sleeve and cries for his mama.

A LADDER THROUGH A TREE

There is nothing dried up
about the cricket limbs
of Celia's earrings, a pair
of skeletons who wait and grin
going up the ladder's rungs,
swaying their heads and hips,
bouncing among the branches,
oranges, and trembling leaves.
Celia is new to fruit picking;
her ladder sways with her steps.

There is nothing dried up
about Celia's dancing twins
waiting for her sack to fill
and for her to climb higher,
trying to reach one more.
Her unbalancing is their joy.
Her hanging silver crickets
sport a smile when they hear
the ladder creak, their music.

GUADALUPE'S HAIR

When Guadalupe wears a hat
and bends to work in a row,
one can't tell if he's a boy or girl.

Once a wind slapped off that hat,
and I saw Guadalupe's hair.
I bet no comb ever made it through.

The top of his head is black
as charcoal ready for a match
and dirty as yanked-out roots.

And Guadalupe's hair has taken
the shape of that straw hat;
it's a kind of hair helmet.

I bet no dirt clod could crack it.
When Guadalupe goes to school
we follow him, pestering like flies.

Boys want to touch it just once,
girls giggle to their circle of friends,
and teachers send him to the nurse.

When Guadalupe walks to the office,
he wears his turtle shell with pride
and gets out of school another day.

SCARECROW II

He walks in the shade of an on-ramp
that veers and merges into a freeway,
an uncoiling snake, the scales of cars
streaming with color and symmetry.
He is bare-footed in a field.
The strips of plastic sheets over
the rows of strawberries undulate,
glaring like church windows.

He plants his feet in the soil.
His body turns to whirling dust.
His robe flutters like a rag.
Only the imprint of His face on the board
and the nails that pierced His palms
are left on the cross, a scarecrow's skeleton.

A field hand, seeing His face, drops
his hoe and walks over to the scarecrow,
calling to his wife, saying: "Mirada."
Another family from a neighboring field
begins to gather around, and on the freeway
a whore in a Camaro recognizes Him,
dropping her cellular phone, and others
start honking, merging into the slow lane.

A sick man being driven taps the dashboard
and says: "Let me out. Stop here. Stop."
His driver expects the worst and pulls over.
The sick man jumps out, climbs a chain-link fence,
and walks to the scarecrow while his driver shouts:
"Where are you going, Ray? Wait for me."

SHE RETURNS

With a mirror in one hand,
she sat at the foot of my bed,
brushing her hair,
black as a frog's eye.

The more she brushed,
the longer her hair grew,
intertwining my legs, my chest.
It rose over me, a river of curls.

She asked why
I called her La Llorona.
I couldn't answer her.
She was tired of my stories.

A face floated by me as I sank.
It was her mirror, holding my face
like a current moving out,
carrying me to darker water.

A rotting bush bordered the dark.
I swam by a pair of pants that kicked,
caged in by the beached branches
that twisted in the currents.

She pointed past the branches,
brushing her hair from her face,
swimming beside me, urging me on,
the water stinging my eyes.

RING

The flashlights roamed, looking for footprints.
When they were caught, they stood, man
and wife, alert as a coyote's ears.

In jail they leaned on the walls
like the mummies of Guanajuato.
A hanging bulb was their moon.

They had spent a honeymoon of planning.
The first time they crossed the border
a marriage of decisions awaited them.

They had found a garage to live in.
Her factory of diapers and stink was across town.
His truck bed of shovels drove him to ditches.

At night the pear-shaped fruit of a cactus
peeled open, blossoming white feathers.
He waited for her near an abandoned car.

Her sandals paused over the broken glass.
A pair of headlights were watchful of her,
attentive as a man saying his vows.

A DAY WORKER AT THE PARK

Today I was without work and waited
with the pigeons, listening to the braking cars,
hoping a new foreman would come for me.
Mothers arrived, pushing their strollers,
stopping at the sandbox's edge, lifting their kids.
I planned for tomorrow, studying my palm
like the fortune teller who traced the border
I crossed to reach El Norte and the villages
I went through on a train that entered a tunnel
long as a nightmare; I knew the direction
I was going, and below my feet the tracks
pounded like a hammer and pointed to the U.S.
At Tijuana I decided to cross the border;
my coyote knew the holes in the wall,
knew the desert's night paths, but he froze
when headlights found our scent and tracked us.
He was part cactus, part shadow, trapped betwee
the pick-up points we had to travel by.

CIRCUIT

The field is a drunkard
who rises, traps me
with his half-lies,
and carries me away
in his need to work off
his hangover and bad luck.

In the field the sun
becomes my husband's eye,
a foreman pushing me
through the rows, asking me
how many baskets I've done.
Later we heat a can of beans
over a fire while the water
in the rows recedes with the dusk.

The field is the weight
of crates we fill, the weight
of being his wife.
In the morning I load his truck
while he stops to listen
to the engine idle.
"What music," he says.
Then we drive
with the field by my side,
reminding me what's ahead.

"Campesina"
Scratchboard, 8"x 12"